Spot
the
Difference

Spot the Difference

100 brand-new puzzles

From Simple Spots to Ultimate Challenges

Quercus

Contents

How to do the puzzles

Soon you'll be having fun like the people in this puzzle! To help you get started, here's a quick run-through of what to look out for.

The number of changes you need to spot is noted here. Remember: those with the most changes are not necessarily the most difficult . . .

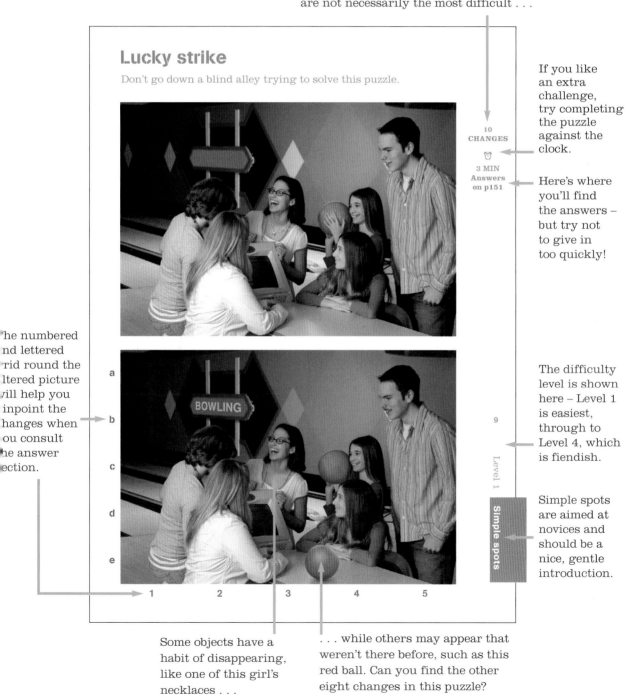

Lucky strike

Don't go down a blind alley trying to solve this puzzle.

10
CHANGES

3 MIN
Answers
on p151

9

Level 1

Simple spots

BOWLING

a
b
c
d
e

1   2   3   4   5

If you like an extra challenge, try completing the puzzle against the clock.

Here's where you'll find the answers – but try not to give in too quickly!

The numbered and lettered grid round the altered picture will help you pinpoint the changes when you consult the answer section.

The difficulty level is shown here – Level 1 is easiest, through to Level 4, which is fiendish.

Simple spots are aimed at novices and should be a nice, gentle introduction.

Some objects have a habit of disappearing, like one of this girl's necklaces . . .

. . . while others may appear that weren't there before, such as this red ball. Can you find the other eight changes in this puzzle?

Simple
spots

Puzzle in the park

These kids are having a swinging time at the park. But take a closer look at the picture on the right and you'll see that things are not always as they should be . . .

Level 1

Simple spots

a
b
c
d
e
f
g
h

1   2   3   4   5   6   7   8

Level 1

Simple spots

In the swim

The race is on to uncover the crafty changes that appear below. But don't go goggle-eyed trying to solve this puzzle!

8 CHANGES

🕐 2 MIN

Answers on p151

a

b

c

d

e

1 2 3 4 5

Breakfast bonanza

Wake up and smell the coffee! Nothing could be simpler than a lovely family breakfast could it? Well, could it?

7
CHANGES

4 MIN
Answers on p151

a
b
c
d
e

1   2   3   4   5

Level 1

Simple spots

Foul play?

The game's just started and we suspect foul play already.
Who's been tampering with the jerseys on the right?

12

Level 1

Simple spots

Now that's healthy!

Six healthy friends have each filled their shopping baskets with the exact same produce at the market – except for one. Can you find the subtle difference below?

2 MIN

Answers on p151

Party poppers?

Let's celebrate! But can you spot the one vital difference between all these balloons before they (or you!) go pop?

🕐

3 MIN

Answers on p151

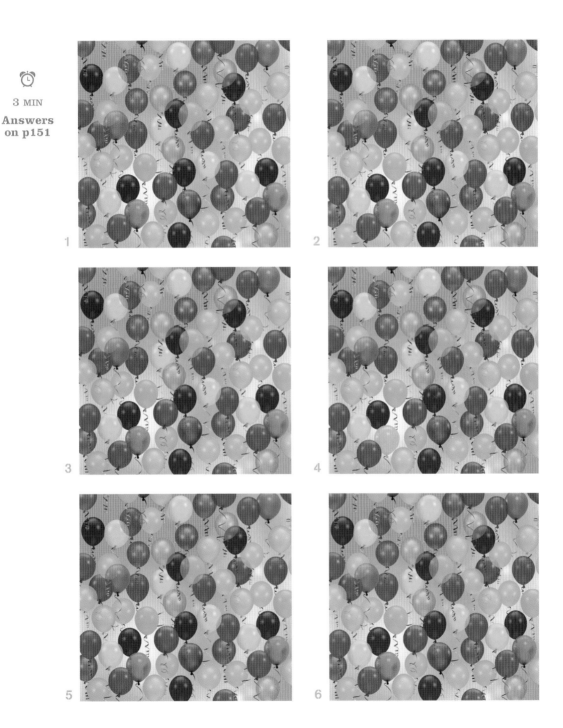

Level 1

Simple spots

Look up, look down

Look all around these delightful domes if you want to locate the hidden differences between the two pictures. The sky's the limit!

a

b

c

d

e

1   2   3   4   5

16

Level 1

Simple spots

Gone fishing

The fishermen may have left the scene but there's definitely a catch (or eight) with this puzzle. What's amiss below?

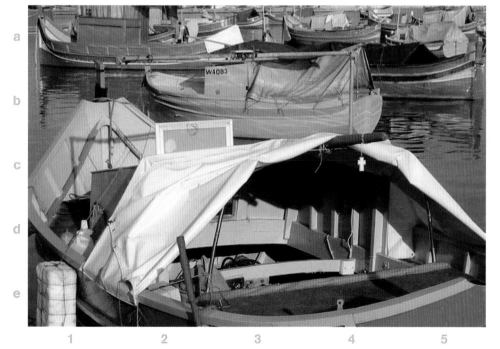

a

b

c

d

e

1   2   3   4   5

Level 1

Simple spots

Watch the birdie!

Don't be fooled by this tranquil scene. If you relax for too long
you may find yourself in a flap!

18

Level 1

a

b

c

d

e

1   2   3   4   5

Dye-ing for a change

What's gone wrong on this vibrant market stall? We only turned our backs for a minute . . .

7
CHANGES

4 MIN

Answers on p151

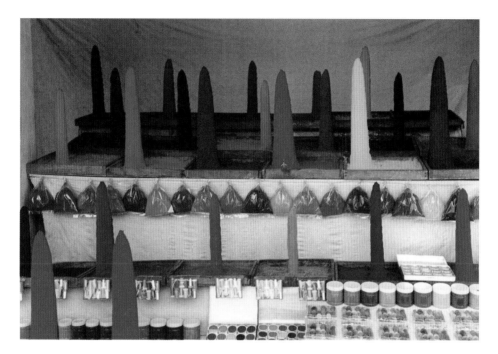

a

b

c

d

e

1   2   3   4   5

Level 1

Simple spots

Yum yum in the sun

The sun's out, but don't stay in the shade for too long – this puzzle needs solving fast!

3 MIN

Answers on p151

Level 1

Simple spots

a

b

c

d

e

1   2   3   4   5

Mamma mia!

There's a prankster loose in the pizzeria. Make sure you spot all the differences before you tuck in.

a

b

c

d

e

1   2   3   4   5

Level 1

Simple spots

Balloon bonanza

This puzzle will leave you flying high – but only if you can solve it in the suggested time limit. Otherwise, you may come down to earth with a bump.

22

a

b

c

d

e

1   2   3   4   5

Bouncing babies

It's a sunny day and these babies seem to be behaving themselves. But can you locate the changes without going gaga? Or even goo-goo?

23

a

b

c

d

e

1   2   3   4   5

Level 1

Simple spots

Home entertainment

Popcorn? Check. Beer? Check. DVD? Check. Everything as it should be? Not in the picture below . . .

a

b

c

d

e

1   2   3   4   5

Level 1

Simple spots

Mad scientists

There's trouble brewing in the lab. And if you can't spot the changes below, this experiment may go badly wrong.

10 CHANGES

5 MIN

Answers on p152

a

b

c

d

e

1   2   3   4   5

Level 1

Simple spots

Caught in the act

There's a hand in every cash register, but a clever trap has been sprung in one. How quickly can you spot it?

1

2

3

4

5

6

Level 1

Simple spots

Curry confusion

Everything you need to make a spicy curry is here – but one of the images below is different from the others. Can you handle the heat?

1

2

3

4

5

6

27

Level 1

Simple spots

Dig deeper

Scratch the surface and you'll see that some changes have been made to the picture at the bottom. Study each image carefully to discover if you can strike it rich in the time allowed.

Level 1

Simple spots

a

b

c

d

e

1   2   3   4   5

Sleepyville

Nothing out of the ordinary going on in this sleepy street – or is there? Look more carefully and you may get a wake-up call.

8
CHANGES

4 MIN

Answers on p152

a

b

c

d

e

1   2   3   4   5

Level 1

Simple spots

Armchair fan

Read her thoughts: 'Not baseball again?' Can you put this poor girl out of her misery by locating the differences below?

Level 1

Simple spots

a

b

c

d

e

1   2   3   4   5

Pipped at the post

As if the race wasn't exciting enough, you have to try to solve the puzzle as well! So study the form carefully before you begin.

7 CHANGES

4 MIN

Answers on p152

Level 1

Simple spots

Head to head

It's tough out there on the field, but we've made it even tougher by introducing some sneaky changes.

8
CHANGES

3 MIN
**Answers
on p152**

Level 1

Simple spots

a

b

c

d

e

1   2   3   4   5

Ring my bell

If you can find the differences below, our Mexican friend will take off his sombrero to you.

33

a

b

c

d

e

1   2   3   4   5

Level 1

Simple spots

Digging for change

This family certainly take their gardening seriously. Which is why they haven't noticed the changes. Can you help them to dig them up?

34

Level 1

Simple spots

Chocoholics

Delicious as it looks, all is not as it seems with the chocolate box below. Can you spot all the differences in the time allowed?

7
CHANGES

3 MIN
Answers on p152

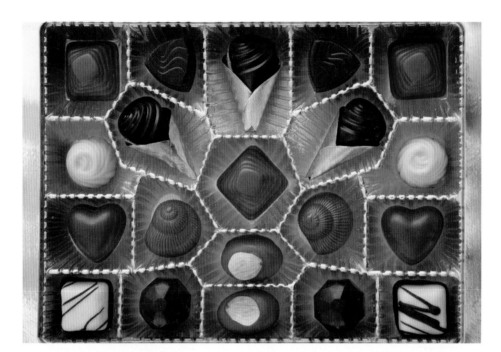

Simple spots

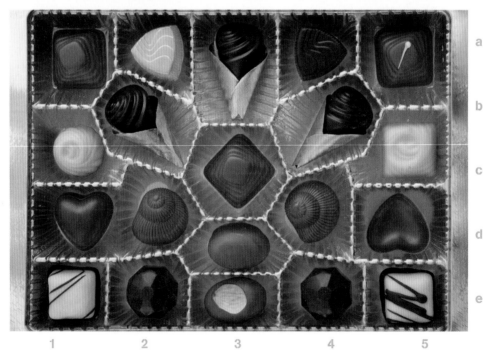

a

b

c

d

e

1   2   3   4   5

Grrrrr!

Underneath this tough exterior is a cuddly little cub. Let's face it
– it shouldn't be hard to uncover the changes made.

8
CHANGES

3 MIN

**Answers
on p153**

a

b

c

d

e

1   2   3   4   5

Level 1

Simple spots

Climbing the wall

One false move and our climber could find herself on the way down. Quick – find the odd one out before she takes a tumble.

3 MIN

Answers on p153

1

2

3

4

Level 1

Simple spots

5

6

Flower girls

This is one of our more fragrant pages – you can almost smell the flowers. But can you spot the one subtle difference?

3 MIN

Answers on p153

1

2

3

4

5

6

Level 1

Simple spots

Viva Las Vegas!

Can you ring the changes in the city that never sleeps? Go on, take a gamble!

40

Level 1

Simple spots

a

b

c

d

e

1   2   3   4   5

Zebra crossing

You'll go wild if you can't solve this puzzle in the time allowed.
Either that or cross-eyed!

Level 1

Simple spots

Flower power

Come on in! Take steps to solve this puzzle in the time allowed.

7
CHANGES

4 MIN
**Answers
on p153**

42

Level 1

Simple spots

Full steam ahead

Try not to lose your train of thought as you steam through this puzzle!

Level 1

Simple spots

a

b

c

d

e

1   2   3   4   5

Snow fun!

This couple are certainly getting their kicks in the snow. Can you find the differences before they complete their run?

3 MIN

Answers on p153

45

a

b

c

d

e

1   2   3   4   5

Simple spots

Brrrrrr!

You've got three minutes before the snowman melts. Can you find all the differences before he becomes a puddle?

8
CHANGES

3 MIN
**Answers
on p153**

Level 1

Simple spots

a

b

c

d

e

1   2   3   4   5

Canoe line-up

Here's your chance to create a splash. Spot the differences before these canoes hit the water.

a

b

c

d

e

1   2   3   4   5

Level 1

Simple spots

Pussycat puzzle

Everyone knows that cats hate water. So help our feline friend to split the scene by finding the changes fast. Miaow!

Level 1

Simple spots

Level 1

Simple spots

Vision vexers

Havana good time?

Searching for the changes should keep you busy. But no cigars if you complete the puzzle in the time allowed!

Level 2

Vision vexers

Level 2

Vision vexers

Bienvenue! Willkommen!

Everyone is welcome at this international hotel – especially if they can identify the changes made to the image at the bottom.

7
CHANGES

3 MIN

Answers on p153

Level 2

Vision vexers

a

b

c

d

e

1   2   3   4   5

Sail away . . .

Anchors aweigh, as we take to the seas for some nautical fun.
Can you spot the differences? Aye, aye captain!

8
CHANGES

4 MIN

**Answers
on p153**

a

b

c

d

e

1   2   3   4   5

Level 2

Vision vexers

Wake up!

There's nothing more civilized than breakfast with friends. Or so we thought until we found out that's not eggs-actly true!

Level 2

Vision vexers

a

b

c

d

e

1   2   3   4   5

Aaaaah!

This is a gentle, relaxing puzzle. So breathe deeply and begin . . .

a

b

c

d

e

1   2   3   4   5

Level 2

Vision vexers

Tile trouble

We know that one of these tiles is slightly different from the others but we don't know where or how. Can you help find the odd tile out?

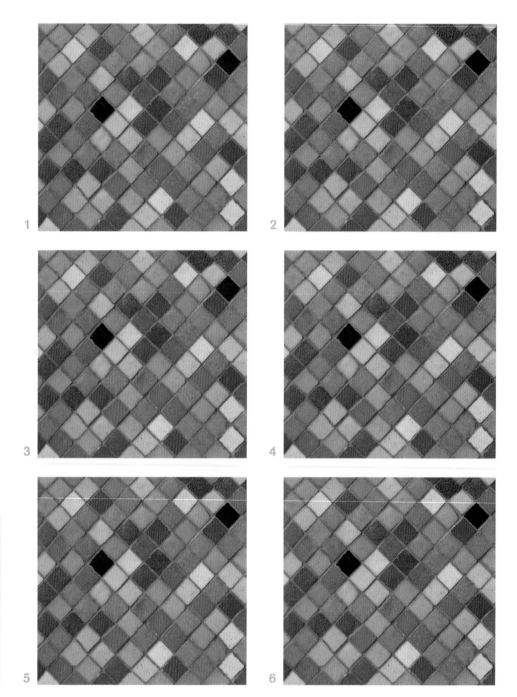

Level 2

Vision vexers

First past the post

It's a photo finish – but what's wrong with one of these pictures of the winning horse? Only the smartest will be able to solve this equestrian teaser?

4 MIN
Answers on p154

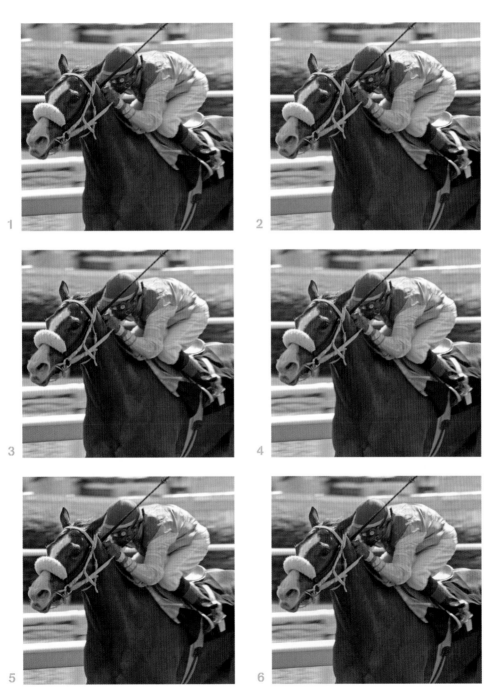

1

2

3

4

5

6

Monster trucks

They're raring to go. Can you spot all the differences before these giant trucks hit the highway?

Level 2

Vision vexers

a

b

c

d

e

1   2   3   4   5

Speed demon

Get ready for the race. If you can find all the changes you should be wheel-y proud!

61

a

b

c

d

e

1   2   3   4   5

Level 2

Vision vexers

Tank teaser

There's certainly something fishy going on here. But if you can spot the differences in the allotted time, everything will go swimmingly.

a

b

c

d

e

1   2   3   4   5

62

Level 2

Vision vexers

Know your onions

Here's a sizzling puzzle. How quickly can you dish up the differences and help the barbecue chef avoid mealtime mayhem?

8
CHANGES

3 MIN
**Answers
on p154**

63

a

b

c

d

e

1   2   3   4   5

Level 2

Vision vexers

Tooty fruity

Picking the right pineapple is a serious business – especially if someone's been messing with the fruit. Help our man spot the differences opposite.

64

a

SALE

b

c

d

e

f

g

h

1   2   3   4   5   6   7   8

Level 2

Vision vexers

A wondrous puzzle

Discover that all is not as it seems in this beautiful image of the Taj Mahal. Reflect for a while then begin.

8 CHANGES

4 MIN

Answers on p154

a b c d e f g h

1 2 3 4 5 6 7 8

67

Level 2

Take a chance

Someone has performed sleight of hand so that the bottom picture no longer matches the top one exactly. Can you put it to rights?

a

b

c

d

e

1   2   3   4   5

Pretty Polly and friends

These pretty little birdies need your help. Can you spot the changes without ruffling your (or their) feathers?

9
CHANGES

5 MIN
Answers on p154

a

b

c

d

e

1   2   3   4   5

Level 2

Vision vexers

Shipping news

This picture is as pretty as a postcard. But can you steer yourself in the right direction to find one little alteration?

Level 2

🕐 4 MIN

Answers on p154

1

2

3

4

5

6

Fancy facades

There are squares here, there and everywhere. But one of these facades differs from the others. Which one?

4 MIN

Answers on p154

1

2

3

4

5

6

Level 2

Vision vexers

Standing to attention

Don't be distracted by the vibrant hues on this page as you search for the changes that appear in the bottom picture.

8
CHANGES

4 MIN
Answers on p155

Level 2

Vision vexers

a

b

c

d

e

1   2   3   4   5

Fly the flag

Put on your helmet and let the battle commence, as you grapple with this noble puzzle.

a

b

c

d

e

1   2   3   4   5

Level 2

Vision vexers

Sightseeing

Forget spotting the sights, and see whether you can spot the differences below instead!

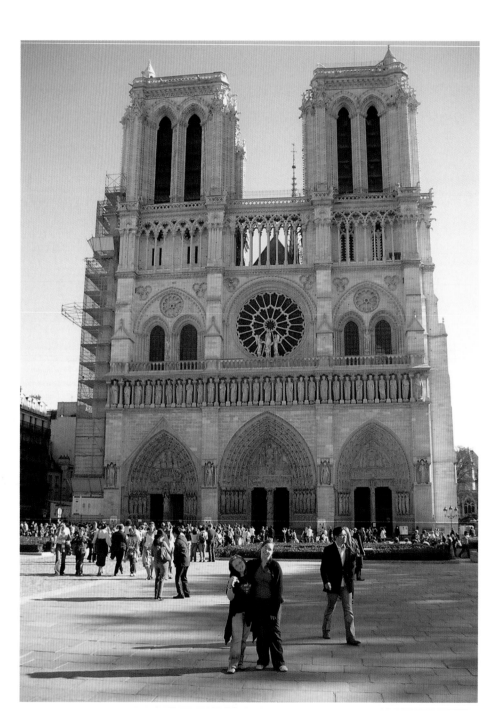

Level 2

Vision vexers

Level 2

Vision vexers

No cheating!

The cards are on the table. But can you complete this puzzle without cheating?

76

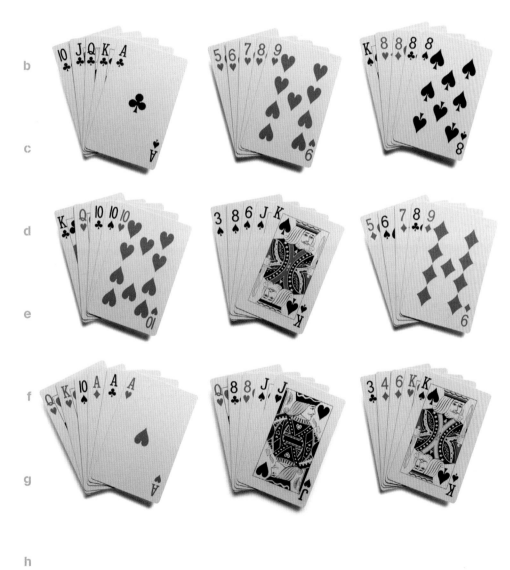

Wedding feast

If you can find all the differences opposite you can enjoy toasting the happy couple.

Level 2

Vision vexers

On the waterfront

There have been some interesting goings-on here at the
waterfront when our backs were turned. Can you spot them?

Level 2

Vision vexers

a

b

c

d

e

1   2   3   4   5

Crowd-pleaser

The stage is set for this puzzle. Sit still and wait for the fun.
You may get a standing ovation if you can complete the
puzzle in time!

9
CHANGES

🕑

5 MIN
**Answers
on p155**

Level 2

Vision vexers

Take a break

Can you imagine a more perfect place for a summer trip? But look closer – is it really as perfect as it seems?

8
CHANGES

🕐
5 MIN

Answers on p155

a b c d e f g h

1 2 3 4 5 6 7 8

Level 2

Vision vexers

American dream

This couple can hardly believe their luck. But will you need luck to solve this puzzle, or can you rely on skill alone?

Level 2

Vision vexers

10
CHANGES

5 MIN

Answers on p155

a

b

c

d

e

1   2   3   4   5

All that glitters . . .

All is not as it seems at this beautiful market stall. Let your eyes wander to the bottom picture as you survey the changes.

9
CHANGES

4 MIN

Answers on p155

a

b

c

d

e

1   2   3   4   5

Level 2

Vision vexers

Fire away!

Don't get too fired up trying to spot the differences in the time allowed. These guys might not be around to help you out!

Level 2

Vision vexers

Mistake by the lake

Blue skies, calm blue waters . . . what could possibly be amiss in this peaceful scene?

Level 2

Vision vexers

Level 2

Vision vexers

Snowy scene

Can you locate the changes in this winter wonderland? First one
to finish gets to build a snowman.

10
CHANGES

5 MIN
**Answers
on p155**

Level 2

Vision vexers

a

b

c

d

e

1   2   3   4   5

What a feast!

Try to find the differences before our twins tuck in to this tasty teatime treat.

9
CHANGES

⏰
4 MIN

Answers
on p155

a

b

c

d

e

1   2   3   4   5

Level 2

Vision vexers

Eye
strainers

Man at work

What do you think – will lots of changes come crawling out of the woodwork? See if you can find them in the allotted time.

Level 3

Eye strainers

**9
CHANGES**

4 MIN

**Answers
on p156**

a

b

c

d

e

1   2   3   4   5

Prickly puzzle

Here's a real prickly pair. What's not as it should be in the bottom picture?

a

b

c

d

e

1   2   3   4   5

Level 3

Eye strainers

Tropical teaser

Can't see the wood for the trees? What's the one difference between all of these pictures?

5 MIN
Answers on p156

1

2

3

4

5

6

Level 3

Eye strainers

Cookie confusion

Don't be dazzled by this sweet selection. Keep your mind focused on finding the one alteration.

5 MIN

Answers on p156

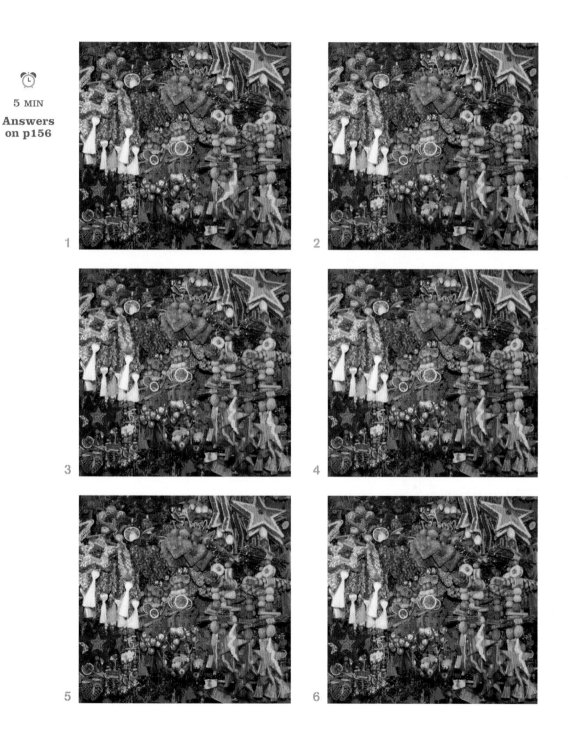

Gridlock

Some days getting home from work can be such a chore. Can you take the fast lane to solve this puzzle?

Level 3

Eye strainers

a

b

c

d

e

1   2   3   4   5

Bubble trouble

We hope this puzzle doesn't burst your bubble! Spot the differences before they float up, up and away.

99

a

b

c

d

e

1   2   3   4   5

Level 3

Eye strainers

Fun in the sun

Sometimes the best way to complete a puzzle is to lie back and relax.

Level 3

Eye strainers

a

b

c

d

e

1   2   3   4   5

Roger Roger

Pilots are looking younger these days aren't they? All's not as it should be in the cockpit.

a

b

c

d

e

1   2   3   4   5

Level 3

Eye strainers

Mask task

This carnival mask hides a number of secrets. Can you uncover them all in the time allowed?

Level 3

Eye strainers

a

b

c

d

e

1   2   3   4   5

Kite-flying conundrum

Time to get out your binoculars to see if you can spot the kite-flying mix-ups below.

a

b

c

d

e

1   2   3   4   5

Level 3

Eye strainers

Sweet surprises

Someone simply couldn't resist temptation. It's a wonder there's anything left for us to use in our puzzle. Can you complete it in the time allowed?

Level 3

Eye strainers

Push the boat out

This gondolier may be too busy singing to notice that some changes have been made. Close your ears and see if you can find them.

Level 3

Eye strainers

a

b

c

d

e

1   2   3   4   5

See plane?

It's plain to see that something's gone wrong in the bottom picture of this sea-plane.

a

b

c

d

e

1   2   3   4   5

Level 3

Eye strainers

Out of puff

No one has the energy to blow up these balloons or find the one crucial difference between these photos. Can you help?

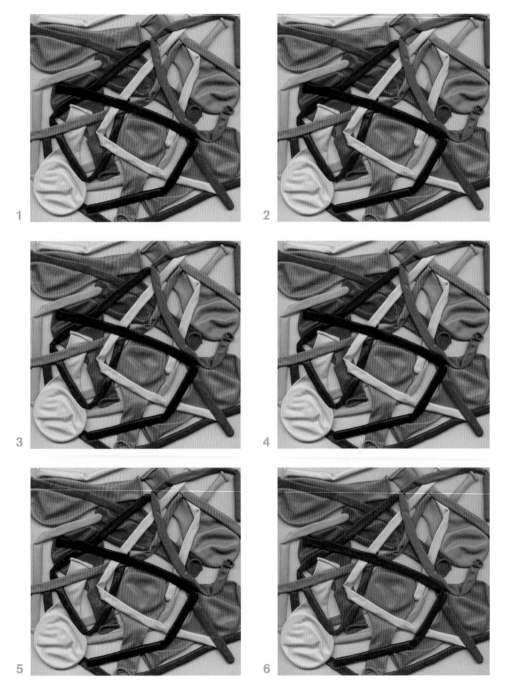

3 MIN

Answers on p156

1

2

3

4

5

6

108

Level 3

Eye strainers

Cute as candy

This puzzle should be as easy as ABC. Which of the pictures differs from the others?

5 MIN

Answers on p157

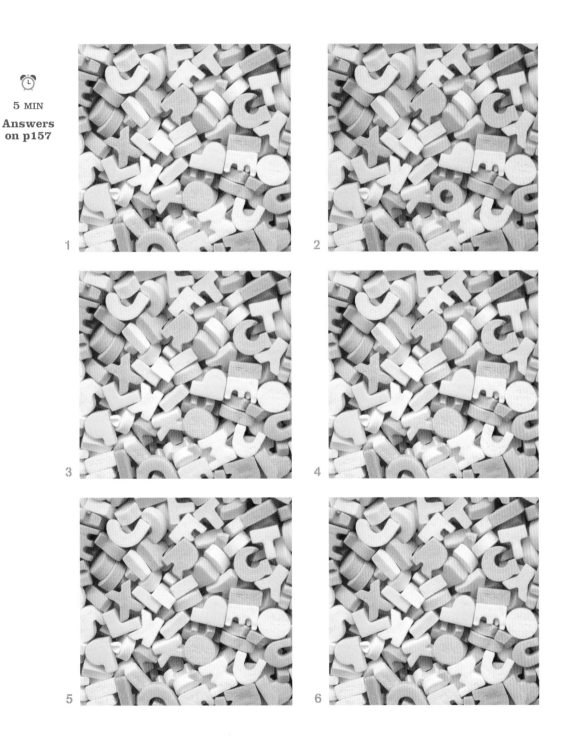

1

2

3

4

5

6

Level 3

Eye strainers

Lassie go home!

If you can't solve this puzzle in the allotted time you may end up with a hang-dog expression!

Level 3

Eye strainers

a

b

c

d

e

1   2   3   4   5

What a catch!

Can you trawl through this puzzle and net yourself some differences?

a

b

c

d

e

1   2   3   4   5

Level 3

Eye strainers

Party time

You may think you're seeing double, triple or even quadruple, but there are some crucial differences between the party on the left and the one on the right.

10
CHANGES

6 MIN

Answers on p157

112

Level 3

Eye strainers

a
b
c
d
e
f
g
h

1 2 3 4 5 6 7 8

Merry-go-round

Don't go round and round in circles trying to solve this puzzle.
Finding the variations between the two pictures shouldn't
make you dizzy.

114

Whatta lotta pots!

Now you have to spot the pot! Throw yourself into this puzzle to
see where the changes have been made.

116

a

b

c

d

e

1   2   3   4   5

Whoa horsey!

Don't jump too fast into this puzzle. Take your time and you may win the rosette.

9
CHANGES

6 MIN
Answers on p157

a

b

c

d

e

1   2   3   4   5

Level 3

Eye strainers

Hill city

You'll need a lot of stamina to get you round the steep inclines of this puzzle.

**8
CHANGES**

7 MIN

**Answers
on p157**

Level 3

Eye strainers

Bright and beautiful

Take a leaf out of our book and find the one variation between these dazzling displays.

7 MIN

Answers on p157

Hip-wiggling fun

We hope that all this shimmying won't distract you from finding the odd one out.

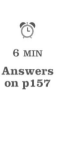

1

2

3

4

5

6

121

Level 3

Eye strainers

Gnome alone

This cheeky little fellow looks like he's been causing mischief in the picture opposite. Can you spot the differences?

122

Level 3

Eye strainers

Ultimate challenges

Hats off

These little dolls just want to be loved. But in the meantime, can you spot the differences between the two pictures?

8
CHANGES

8 MIN

Answers on p157

Level 4

Ultimate challenges

a

b

c

d

e

f

g

h

1   2   3   4   5   6   7   8

Level 4

Ultimate challenges

Super structure

Someone's been tampering with the blueprints. Can you spot the building booboos?

a

b

c

d

e

1   2   3   4   5

Level 4

Ultimate challenges

Chief big mistake

Be brave! This puzzle is fiendishly difficult, but can you work out how, where and why this totem pole has gone wrong?

8
CHANGES

7 MIN
Answers on p158

a

b

c

d

e

1   2   3   4   5

Level 4

Ultimate challenges

Good year!

Ring the changes with a good bottle of wine! But before you pop the cork, which picture is the odd one out?

8 MIN

Answers on p158

130

Jellybean genius

Spot the odd jellybean out if you want to take the title!

⏰

9 MIN

**Answers
on p158**

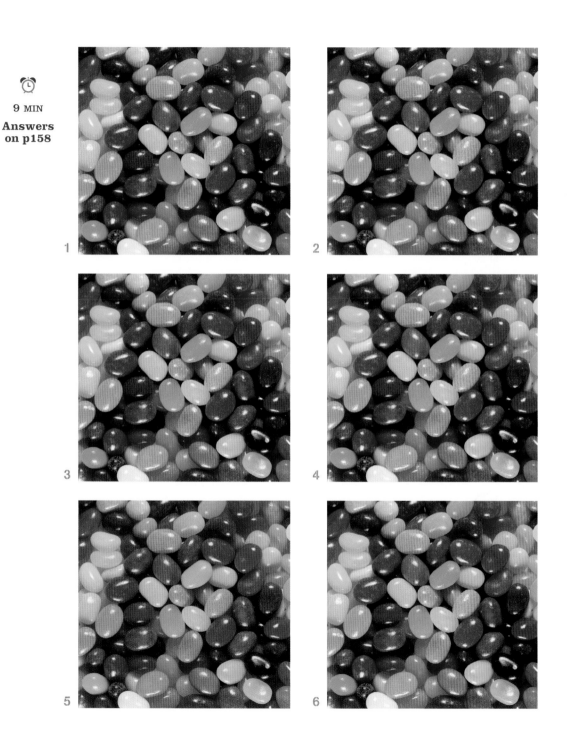

1

2

3

4

5

6

Level 4

Ultimate challenges

Weird Christmas

Where's the Christmas spirit here? Some of the toys below are not at all happy. Look closely to see if you can discover why.

10
CHANGES

9 MIN
Answers on p158

Level 4

Ultimate challenges

Level 4

Ultimate challenges

Temple trouble

You'll be blowing your own trumpet if you can spot what's gone wrong in this decorative disaster.

10
CHANGES

10 MIN

Answers on p158

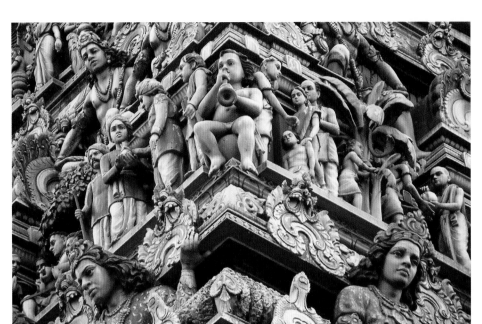

134

Level 4

Ultimate challenges

a

b

c

d

e

1   2   3   4   5

Excess baggage

Someone doesn't travel light, that's for sure! Find out why there may be chaos at the airport in the picture below.

135

Level 4

Ultimate challenges

Pick out the penguin

Stick your beak in and see if you can spot the odd one out in this perplexing penguin parade.

Level 4

Ultimate challenges

Pebbles on the beach

Leave no stone unturned in trying to solve this puzzle. Which
stony scene is different from the others?

8 MIN

**Answers
on p158**

Level 4

Ultimate challenges

You're getting warm

Don't let your senses desert you. Everything on this sunny island paradise is not as it seems.

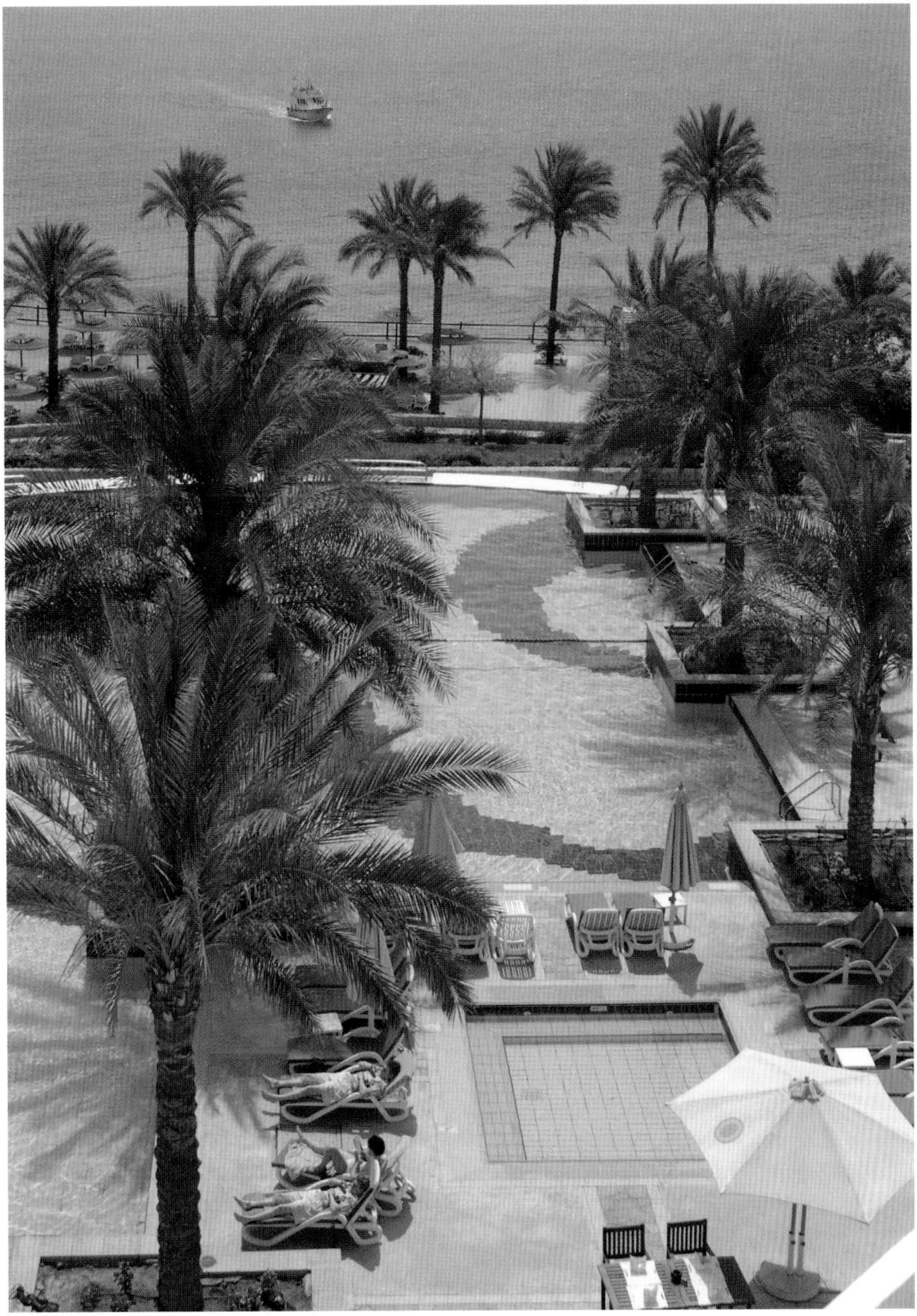
a
b
c
d
e
f
g
h
1
2
3
4
5
6
7
8

Room with a view

Rooftops as far as the eye can see. But can you spot the differences in the bottom picture from your vantage point?

10
CHANGES

12 MIN

Answers on p158

Level 4

Tough science

You don't have to be good at science to solve this puzzle – but a sharp pair of eyes will help you decipher this molecular mayhem.

9
CHANGES

10 MIN
Answers on p158

Level 4

Ultimate challenges

a

b

c

d

e

f

g

h

1   2   3   4   5   6   7   8

143

Touching the sky

Get your head out of the clouds – there's a small but crucial difference in one of these pictures. Can you spot it?

1

2

9 MIN

Answers on p158

3

4

5

6

Level 4

Ultimate challenges

Don't stall for time

There's something off here. Which of these is the imposter?

9 MIN

Answers on p158

Level 4

Ultimate challenges

On parade

The palace requests that you do your best to complete this regal puzzle. We hope that you are amused.

a

b

c

d

e

1   2   3   4   5

Level 4

Ultimate challenges

Shirts off

Nothing could be simpler than trying to find a shirt and tie that match. Or could it?

10
CHANGES

10 MIN
**Answers
on p159**

a
b
c
d
e

1   2   3   4   5

Level 4

Ultimate challenges

Busy beach

It's confusing when everyone decides to hit the beach at the same time. See if you can help clear the scene.

148

a

b

c

d

e

1   2   3   4   5

Level 4

Ultimate challenges

The curtain falls

The last puzzle in the book is the hardest of all. Only those with beady eyes will be able to solve it.

8
CHANGES

🕐

13 MIN

Answers on p159

a
b
c
d
e

1   2   3   4   5

Level 4

Ultimate challenges

Answers

How to do the puzzles

P5: Lucky strike No. 1 (A1) We've lost a diamond at the back. No. 2 (B2–B3) BOWLING has appeared from nowhere. No. 3 (B3) One diamond is now green. No. 4 (B5) This man has a new moustache. No. 5 (C3) Someone's lost a necklace. No. 6 (C4) Where's her hand gone? No. 7 (C5) He's got a new red button. No. 8 (E1) From green stripes to blue. No. 9 (E3–E4) That ball wasn't there before. No. 10 (E4) Her sleeve is now green, not purple.

Simple spots

P8: Puzzle in the park No. 1 (A6) Someone's hand is missing. No. 2 (D3) There's a new logo on his t-shirt. No. 3 (F1–F2). A piece of wood is missing. No. 4 (F4–F6) The girl's skirt has grown longer. No. 5 (F4–H5) Her tights now have polka dots. No. 6 (H2–H8) The red pole is now green. No. 7 (H7) A red triangle has appeared.

P10: In the swim No. 1 (A3–A4) The 8 has changed to a 9. No. 2 (A5) A third foot has appeared. No. 3 (B4) The goggles have changed from black to blue. No. 4 (B5) The swimmer on the right is wearing a red cap not a yellow one. No. 5 (C3) These arm-straps weren't there before. No. 6 (C4) The swimming costume has an extra strap. No. 7 (D3) A red float has disappeared. No. 8 (E5) Quick, get out of the water! That fin wasn't there before.

P11: Breakfast bonanza No. 1 (C2) The girl has a flower in her hair. No. 2 (C3) We've lost the back of the chair. No. 3 (D1) The flower has lost its bottom leaf. No. 4 (D3) The orange juice has become milk. No. 5 (D4) Mum's zipper is now black. No. 6 (E4) The top of the pot has disappeared. No. 7 (E5) There's an extra jug here that wasn't there before.

P12: Foul play? No. 1 (A6–B8) The jersey on the end is now orange and not red. No. 2 (B4–B5) The middle number has grown. No. 3 (C1) The stripe on the far left arm is now yellow. No. 4 (D4–D5) Someone has moved the logo on the middle jersey from right to left. No. 5 (E8) The far right double stripe is now a triple stripe. No. 6 (F4–F5) A 3 has become a 9. No. 7 (G4) We've lost a 1 on the arm in the middle. No. 8 (H8) A logo has vanished on the last jersey.

P14: Now that's healthy! In photo No. 5 the apple at the front is now completely red rather than red and yellow.

P15: Party poppers? The orange balloon at the bottom left corner of photo No. 4 is now pink.

P16: Look up, look down No. 1 (A4) The pole has grown longer. No. 2 (B3) Someone's turned one of the decorative objects upside down. No. 3 (C2) And another one has disappeared completely. No. 4 (C4) The square structure at the side of the big dome has vanished. No. 5 (D2) We've gained an extra dome on top of a plinth. No. 6 (D5) One of the carved decorations has increased in size. No. 7 (E5) One of the little decorations has gone from the side.

P17: Gone fishing No. 1 (A1) The yellow stripe on the boat has become orange. No. 2 (B2) The S has become a W. No. 3 (B2–C2) We've lost a pole completely here. No. 4 (B5) A cloth has vanished from the side of a boat. No. 5 (C4) The cross has increased in size. No. 6 (D2–E2) This pole has got longer. No. 7 (E1) The pack at the side of the boat is now yellow. No. 8 (E5) A yellow strip of wood has been removed from the boat.

P18: Watch the birdie! No. 1 (A1) An extra bird is in the sky. No. 2 (A4) This bird is now flying in the opposite direction. No. 3 (A5) This tree has grown quickly. No. 4 (B1) There's an extra boat on the lake. No. 5 (B4) This boat now has a sail. No. 6 (C1) A little bird has vanished. No. 7 (C4) One of the posts is shorter. No. 8 (C5) From white bird to pink bird. No. 9 (D4–E4) The swan now has a dark back.

P19: Dye-ing for a change No. 1 (A3–B3) An extra dome of dye has appeared at the back. No. 2 (A5–C5) The yellow dome has moved to the right. No. 3 (C1) A red packet has disappeared. No. 4 (C3) The orange packet is now red. No. 5 (E2) One of the jars has gained a label. No. 6 (E4–E5) A packet at the front has disappeared. No. 7 (E5) A white lid has become a red lid.

P20: Yum yum in the sun No. 1 (A2) An extra tree's appeared in the background. No. 2 (B3–C3) The little girl has grown an extra pigtail. No. 3 (B4) A tree's disappeared here. No. 4 (C4–D4) The girl on the right's top is now dark pink. No. 5 (D2) This plate's no longer empty. No. 6 (D5) Part of the basket handle has vanished.

P21: Mamma mia! No. 1 (A2) The spring onions have lost a band. No. 2 (A2) A slice of onion has appeared from nowhere. No. 3 (A4–A5) One of the jars has a label that wasn't there before. No. 4 (B4) Someone's eaten a slice of salami. No. 5 (C1–C2) And a slice of pizza! No. 6 (C3) There's an extra mushroom. No. 7 (D3) A little bit of salami is missing from the pizza. No. 8 (D4–D5) The stalk on the pepper has changed direction.

P22: Balloon bonanza No. 1 (A4) Some letters have disappeared. No. 2 (C3) The white section of this balloon has continued right round. No. 3 (C5) We've got an upside-down crown. No. 4 (D1–D2) The car's roof is now black. No. 5 (D3) A woman has disappeared. No. 6 (D4) We've lost a dark stripe on the right. No. 7 (E2) The red car has lost its number plate. No. 8 (E3–E4) An orange light has become a yellow light.

P23: Bouncing babies No. 1 (B3) The buggy's handle has vanished. No. 2 (C1) The man in the white hat has disappeared. No. 3 (C3) The chin-strap on this little baby's hat has gone. No. 4 (C4) The woman's backless top covers more of her back now. No. 5 (C4) The red stripe on the baby's hat has become a yellow stripe. No. 6 (D2) The pink circle has become a pink triangle. No. 7 (D4–D5) A blue triangle has appeared on the mat.

P24: Home entertainment No. 1 (A3) A light has been removed. No. 2 (B1) One of the wires on the hanging object has disappeared. No. 3 (C4) The DVD cover looks different. No. 4 (D2) Her top covers her more. No.5 (D5) The cushion is now blue. No. 6 (E4) The candle's grown bigger.

P25: Mad scientists No. 1 (A4) The 6 on the clock has vanished. No. 2 (B1) One of the cupboards now has a handle. No. 3 (B3) A bottle behind has disappeared. No. 4 (B4) This woman's hair has been trimmed on one side. No. 5 (C4) Her lab coat has a new badge. No. 6 (D1) His coat now has a pocket. No. 7 (D3) Part of his syringe has disappeared. No. 8 (E1) The test-tube on the left has vanished. No. 9 (E2) One of the blue liquids has changed to orange. No. 10 (E3) The circular object in front has gone.

P26: Caught in the act In photo No. 2 the big button at the bottom looks different.

P27: Curry confusion In photo No. 5 the big tub in the background has a blue lid rather than a pink lid.

P28: Dig deeper No. 1 (A3) Something red has appeared from nowhere at the top. No. 2 (B1–C1) The central gap has disappeared. No. 3 (C5–D5) An extra arm has appeared at the end of the row. No. 4 (D1–E1) The structure in the background has vanished. No. 5 (D2) A red component has become a black component. No. 6 (E4) The plinth has grown longer.

P29: Sleepyville No. 1 (A3–B3) Part of the wall has changed from orange to purple. No. 2 (C2–E2) The line in the middle of the road wasn't there before. No. 3 (C1–D1) All of the timbers on the left have been removed. No. 4 (C3) Whoever heard of a red bush? No. 5 (D2) This lantern has been extended out. No. 6 (D3) The red car has become a blue car. No. 7 (E1) There's an extra chimney on the roof. No. 8 (E3–E4) The slanting section of the roof has gone.

P30: Armchair fan No. 1 (A4) One hand on the clock is now pointing to the 4, not the 2. No. 2 (B3) The man is now holding a yellow ball. No. 3 (B5) A curled section on the lamp has disappeared. No. 4 (C4) The remote control has fallen onto his leg. No. 5 (D5) There's an extra beer under the table. No. 6 (E2) The girl has an extra ankle strap. No. 7 (E4) Someone's repaired the hole in his trousers. No. 8 (E5) Part of the table leg has disappeared.

P31: Pipped at the post No. 1 (A5) Someone's planted an extra bush. No. 2 (B1) The white car has become a yellow car. No. 3 (B2) What was UK is now UC. No. 4 (C1) The leading horse now has a nose-guard. No. 5 (C4) An extra horse has joined in. No. 6 (E2) the man in brown trousers has moved to the left. No. 7 (E4) That yellow stripe is new.

P32: Head to head No. 1 (B3) An extra helmet has appeared. No. 2 (C3) A red arm has become a blue arm. No. 3 (C5) One guy's got a logo on his thigh. No. 4 (D1) Someone's got a new bracelet. No. 5 (D1–E2) The single stripe has become a double stripe. No. 6 (D2) The white rectangle is now yellow. No. 7 (D3) The ball's not red any more. No. 8 (D5) Someone's lost a leg.

P33: Ring my bell No. 1 (A2) A blue tassle has become a yellow tassle. No. 2 (B2–B3) The man's moustache has grown even longer. No. 3 (C2) There's a new patch on his shoulder. No. 4 (C3) He's lost the top pot. No. 5 (C4) The chain on his bell is longer. No. 6 (E1–E2) His cuff is now striped. No. 7 (E2–E3) There's a bell in the pot that wasn't there before.

P34: Digging for change No. 1 (A2) A pillar has vanished. No. 2 (A7–A8) The bush on the right now has yellow leaves. No. 3 (C3) That plantpot is new. No. 4 (C7–D8) The boy's red handle is now blue. No. 5 (E8) And his trousers have grown. No. 6 (G3–G4) Dad's shoe looks different. No. 7 (G8) A plant's grown in the pot on the right. No. 8 (H8) An extra flowerpot's appeared.

P36: Chocoholics No. 1 (A2) A dark chocolate has become white. No. 2 (A5) Someone has added a white chocolate stripe. No. 3 (B5–C5) The white chocolate on the right is now square. No. 4 (C2–D2) One of the divider lines of the box has vanished. No. 5 (D3) Someone's eaten one of the almonds from the top. No. 6 (D4–D5) The heart on the right is upside-down. No. 7 (E1) We've lost a dark chocolate stripe.

P37: Grrrrr! No. 1 (B3) One of the black stripes on the tiger's forehead has gone. No. 2 (B3) And one of the white stripes has been shortened. No. 3 (C2) A white stripe has changed to black. No. 4 (D3) Some little black spots have appeared. No. 5 (D3) From pink nose to red. No. 6 (D3) Where's that tooth gone? No. 7 (E3) The black outline of his bottom lip has turned red. No. 8 (E5–D5) The stripe on the cuff of his jersey has disappeared.

P38: Climbing the wall In photo No. 1 one trouser leg is longer than the other.

P39: Flower girls In photo No. 2, a prominent flower on the right has changed from white to yellow.

P40: Viva Las Vegas! No. 1 (B3) A light's gone from the middle of the picture. No. 2 (C1) Part of the long, diagonal light has gone. No. 3 (C2) Someone's extended one of the neon signs as far as the 'R' above it. No. 4 (C2–D2) There's an extra flashing star. No. 5 (C2) A light has slipped down to the bottom of its rectangle. No. 6 (D2–D3) Has that tree grown? No. 7 (D4) Who'd want full-price margaritas? No. 8 (D5) The yellow section is now blue.

P41: Zebra crossing No. 1 (B2) One of the bushes has grown a lot. No. 2 (C2) One of the zebras looks very grey. No. 3 (C3) And another has had a change of direction. No. 4 (C5) Surely there's an extra zebra here? No. 5 (C5) Look closely – the tail has vanished from the zebra on the right. No. 6 (D1) There's an extra bush on the left.

P42: Flower power No. 1 (A1–C1) The black drainpipe has become green. No. 2 (B5) Some of the flowers have vanished. No. 3 (D7) Someone must be expecting bigger packages – the letterbox has grown. No. 4 (F6) Where's the mat? No. 5 (F7) Is that an extra flowerpot? No. 6 (G4–H6) A diagonal rail has disappeared. No. 7 (H6) Some yellow flowers have changed to pink.

P44: Full steam ahead No. 1 (A1–B1) The funnel has been cut short. No. 2 (A3) The gold funnel is now wider. No. 3 (A3) The red pipe is much longer. No. 4 (C1) We've lost a chain. No. 5 (C4) The green component has turned blue. No. 6 (D5) A lever has been removed. No. 7 (E1) A rivet's gone missing. No. 8 (E3–E4) Who's taken the words? No. 9 (E4) This gold band looks much duller.

P45: Snow fun! No. 1 (B2) The woman's white polo neck is now yellow. No. 2 (B3) Has his hair grown? No. 3 (B3) The black square on his lapel has vanished. No. 4 (C1) Someone's taken her ski pole. No. 5 (C3) A white section of his jacket is now black. No. 6 (C3) And he's lost his bottom button. No. 7 (D4–D5) His pole is shorter. No. 8 (E4) That ski is new.

P46: Brrrrr! No. 1 (A2–B2) We've lost a tree at the back. No. 2 (B2) The girl's hat has shrunk. No. 3 (B3) Dad's hat has a new logo. No. 4 (B4) One of the snowman's eyes has moved. No. 5 (B5) And his arm on the right looks different. No. 6 (C4) The snowman has an extra button. No. 7 (E1) The girl's red glove is now blue. No. 8 (E2–E3) Dad's cuff is shorter.

P47: Canoe line-up No. 1 (A1–C1) The left canoe is gone. No. 2 (A2) The red canoe has shrunk. No. 3 (A4–E4) The 4th canoe from right has been turned right round. No. 4 (A5–B5) The green canoe is now blue. No. 5 (B3) Some black lines have vanished on the little orange canoe. No. 6 (B5) This seating space looks different. No. 7 (C2) A yellow canoe has lost a circle. No. 8 (D5) The seating space has changed shape.

P48: Pussycat puzzle No. 1 (A5) The cat has a black patch below its eye on the right. No. 2 (C1–C2) We've grown some extra blue flowers. No. 3 (D5) The black patch on pussy's paw is new. No. 4 (E1) There's an extra leaf in the water. No. 5 (F4) The cat's reflection has gained a black patch. No. 6 (G1–G3) A leaf in the water has turned round. No. 7 (G8–H8) One of the leaves has disappeared.

Vision vexers

P52: Havana good time? No. 1 (A7) A light has disappeared. No. 2 (C5) Was that person there before? No. 3 (F3) The person in the red top's vanished. No. 4 (F5–F6) The child's top is now orange. No. 5 (G3) We've got an extra sticker on the windscreen. No. 6 (G6) A side light has gone missing. No. 7 (G7) There's an extra number plate against the wall.

P54: Bienvenue! Willkommen! No. 1 (A1) One of the window carvings has gone missing. No. 2 (A3) The stone face looks different. No. 3 (A5) The row of bricks has been extended. No. 4 (C1) A flag has changed from red and yellow to plain red. No. 5 (C4) What was a white cross is now a white circle. No. 6 (C5) And what was a green stripe is now blue. No. 7 (D1) Where's that light gone?

P55: Sail away . . . No. 1 (A3) We've lost a cloud in the sky. No. 2 (C2) The red object in the distance is now a bigger blue object. No. 3 (C2) An extra boat has appeared on the horizon. No. 4 (C4) Where did the blue van go? No. 5 (D5) There's a new yellow section on this boat. No. 6 (D5) An extra blue box has also appeared. No. 7 (E1) A new post has appeared at the front. No. 8 (E4) One of the boats now has a name.

P56: Wake up! No. 1 (A1) The back of the chair has vanished. No. 2 (A3) Someone's got a new ring. No. 3 (A5) The plant has moved. No. 4 (A5) And the rim of the plate is red not blue. No. 5 (B3) An extra eggcup has appeared. No. 6 (C4) A cup has lost a handle. No. 7 (C5) Is that a new hairband? No. 8 (D3) A grape's been eaten. No. 9 (D4–E4) A sleeve is longer. No. 10 (E2) Was that grape there before? No. 11 (E2) Someone's added milk to a black coffee.

P57: Aaaaah! No. 1 (A5–B5) There's a dividing line on the stone tile that wasn't there before. No. 2 (B2) A leaf has been removed from this flower. No. 3 (B3) An extra flower has been added to the footbath. No. 4 (B4) A large petal has vanished. No. 5 (D2) A shell has also disappeared. No. 6 (E1–E2) The other shell has turned round. No. 7 (E4–E5) One of the tiles has lost its pattern. No. 8 (E5) The middle part of one flower is now yellow.

P58: Tile trouble In photo No. 2, halfway down on the left, a red tile has become a purple tile.

P59: First past the post The odd one out is photo No. 6 – part of the white line is missing on the saddle.

P60: Monster trucks No. 1 (A5–B5) Someone's added an extra pipe on the right. No. 2 (B2) One of the exhaust pipes has been shortened here. No. 3 (B3) And one has been elongated. No. 4 (B3–B4) The red box at the top has changed to blue. No. 5 (B5) There's an extra orange light. No. 6 (C3) There's also a badge that wasn't there before. No. 7 (C4) Surely that mirror's got bigger? No. 8 (D1–D2) One of the black squares on the front has been removed.

P61: Speed demon No. 1 (C2) Where's the number 2 gone? No. 2 (C3) The white pole has vanished. No. 3 (D1) That hill looks steeper than before. No. 4 (D1) The black numbers look shorter. No. 5 (D2) A new yellow logo has appeared. No. 6 (D3) The remaining white pole has a new black stripe. No. 7 (E2–E3) There's something in the background that wasn't there before. No. 8 (E4) A diagonal bike spoke is missing at the bottom.

P62: Tank teaser No. 1 (A1) One pointed section of the plant is taller. No. 2 (A5) The top fin looks different. No. 3 (B3) There's a yellow fish swimming in the opposite direction. No. 4 (C1) One fish has lost a stripe. No. 5 (C4–C5) A yellow tail has become a white tail. No. 6 (E3) A pink stone has become a purple stone. No. 7 (E5) One of the fish has swum away.

P63: Know your onions No. 1 (A2–A3) The blue cloth is now purple. No. 2 (A4–A5) The fish slice has been removed. No. 3 (B4) There's a handle here that's grown. No. 4 (C1) We've lost a slice of onion. No. 5 (D4–E4) A slice of pepper on the kebab has changed from green to red. No. 6 (E1) The knife handle is now dark blue. No. 7 (E1) A slice of green pepper has vanished. No. 8 (E2–E3) An extra little onion has appeared.

P64: Tooty fruity No. 1 (A1–A2) The sale's just started in the second picture No. 2 (A8) Part of the display is missing top right. No. 3 (C4) Where's his moustache? No. 4 (D2–D5) The big stripe on his jumper is no longer grey. No. 5 (E7) The top of the pineapple looks different. No. 6 (G8) An extra banana has appeared. No. 7 (H5–H7) Some yellow apples are now red apples.

P66: A wondrous puzzle No. 1 (B1) Part of the building showing on the left has vanished. No. 2 (B3) A middle ring has disappeared on the column on the left. No. 3 (B5–C5) We have three domed windows instead of two. No. 4 (B6) This tower looks bigger. No. 5 (E3) Someone's moved closer to the water's edge. No. 6 (E7) We've lost a tree. No. 7 (E7–G8) An extra person has snuck in on the right. No. 8 (H4) A plantpot has turned yellow.

P68: Take a chance No. 1 (A1) Some chips have appeared on the shelf. No. 2 (A3–A4) Part of her necklace has disappeared. No. 3 (B2) This man's tie has changed to red. No. 4 (C2) Some blue chips have become yellow. No. 5 (C4) There's an extra pile of blue chips. No. 6 (C4) This man's cuff is now white. No. 7 (C5) She's got an extra shoulder strap. No. 8 (D3) This card now has six symbols. No. 9 (D3) A circle on the table has disappeared. No. 10 (D4 This woman's gained a new ring. No. 11 (E2) Some cards have disappeared from the edge of the table. No. 12 (E4) A pile of green chips has increased.

P69: Pretty Polly and friends No. 1 (A3) We've lost a long leaf. No. 2 (A4–A5) This parrot now has an orange head. No. 3 (A5) BIRDPARK has changed to BIRDPORK. No. 4 (C1) We've lost another leaf. No. 5 (D1–E1) And there's a leaf here that wasn't there before. No. 6 (D2) One poor parrot's lost a foot. No. 7 (E3) There are some new pink flowers. No. 8 (E4–E5) One of the branches is shorter. No. 9 (E5) An extra little yellow bird has appeared.

P70: Shipping news Photo No. 4 has a red ring on the boat on the right – all the others have a black ring.

P71: Fancy facades Photo No. 3 is missing one of three bricks below the window on the middle right.

P72: Standing to attention No. 1 (B1–B2) There's an extra branch. No. 2 (B3) Something's missing from the branches of the tree. No. 3 (C1) The house has a short new chimney. No. 4 (C3–D3) The pink and blue dress is now orange. No. 5 (C5–D5) The tree trunk in the background has moved a little. No. 6 (D2–E2) The little boy is facing in the opposite direction. No. 7 (D4) The girl in purple's beads are now longer. No. 8 (E2) Someone's lost an ankle bracelet.

P73: Fly the flag No. 1 (A1) The man in red has moved back. No. 2 (B1–C1) A red tunic is now a blue tunic. No. 3 (B2) One warrior now has dark hair. No. 4 (B3) A rider has disappeared. No. 5 (B3–C3) One horse no longer has a white nose. No. 6 (B3–D3) The flagpole just got shorter. No. 7 (B4) One warrior has lost his nose-guard. No. 8 (C4) The white horse has an extra strap. No. 9 (C4–C5) A shield is smaller. No. 10 (C5) A silver helmet has turned black.

P74: Sightseeing No. 1 (B5) An extra spire has appeared. No. 2 (C5) We've lost the rooftop showing through. No. 3 (D5) The middle statue has vanished. No. 4 (F3) One door is taller. No. 5 (G4) The girl's t-shirt logo has disappeared. No. 6 (G6) The man now has a red shirt. No. 7 (G8) A person has been removed at the back. No. 8 (H5) One of the woman's shoes is now brown.

P76: No cheating! No. 1 (B7) The heart has swapped with the diamond. No. 2 (C2) The ace of clubs has become the ace of spades. No. 3 (D1) A king is now a queen. No. 4 (D4) A spade is missing. No. 5 (D6) A heart is now a diamond. No. 6 (E4–E5) The band on the king's crown is now black. No. 7 (F1–G1) There's an extra card. No. 8 (F5–G5) We have a black heart card. No. 9 (F6) The 2 has become 3. No. 10 (F7–G8) The king's V section is yellow.

P78: Wedding feast No. 1 (B5–B6) Those glasses are new. No. 2 (C2) The bride's lost part of her veil. No. 3 (D3) And she now has a flower on her bodice. No. 4 (D8) A pink flower has gone from the cake. No. 5 (F8) There are extra yellow flowers on the cake. No. 6 (H2) A purple flower has vanished. No. 7 (H4–H5) One leaf is now bigger.

P80: On the waterfront No. 1 (A1–B1) One pole is longer. No. 2 (B1) CUSTOMS has disappeared. No. 3 (B3) A side window has disappeared. No. 4 (B4–B5) The pink semi-circle is taller. No. 5 (C1–D1) The boat is pointing the other way. No. 6 (C3–C4) A row of windows has disappeared. No. 7 (C4) The green building is now purple. No. 8 (C5–D5) One of the umbrellas now has more red in it.

P81: Crowd-pleaser No. 1 (A4) A pillar has gone. No. 2 (B2) The gold section of the pillar is longer. No. 3 (B2) Someone has left the building. No. 4 (B5–C5) A woman is now in a pink top. No. 5 (D1–E1) The bench has moved forward. No. 6 (D2) There's someone new in the entrance. No. 7 (E2) Something's missing at the base of the pillar. No. 8 (E2–E3) A new object is here. No. 9 (E3) Someone's changed tabard.

P82: Take a break No. 1 (A7) Work on the dome must be finished. No. 2 (B1) A building is now orange. No. 3 (C1–D1) We've lost a pole. No. 4 (D4) A prominent bush is no longer there. No. 5 (F2) There's something new at the edge. No. 6 (F4) There's an extra boat on the water. No. 7 (G7–H8) The blue cover is now a red cover. No. 8 (H6) We've lost a white jeep.

P84: American dream No. 1 (A1) There's a new chimney. No. 2 (A3–B3) The middle window has a new divider. No. 3 (A4–B4) That window looks different. No. 4 (B2–C2) Half a window has vanished. No. 5 (B5) And so has part of the gutter. No. 6 (C1) We've lost part of the fencepost. No. 7 (C3) What was a black t-shirt is now a grey t-shirt. No. 8 (C4) The flag has gone. No. 9 (E2) A trouser pocket has disappeared. No. 10 (E5) Some more flowers have sprouted.

P85: All that glitters . . . No. 1 (A2) A green scarf is now red. No. 2 (C1) This hat has lost its white stripe. No. 3 (C1) The gold hat has a new logo. No. 4 (C2) There are two stripes on this hat, not one. No. 5 (C4) Someone's lost a watch. No. 6 (D2) She's lost a row of coins on her hip-belt. No. 7 (D3) This pile of hats just got shorter. No. 8 (D3) One shelf is no longer empty. No. 9 (E4) The white hat looks different.

P86: Fire away! No. 1 (B1–A2) A branch has vanished. No. 2 (B7) A light has disappeared. No. 3 (C5) The E has become an F. No. 4 (C6) Was this helmet always yellow? No. 5 (C8–D8) A mailbox has gone. No. 6 (D2–E1) A section of yellow hose has vanished. No. 7 (D3) A leg stripe has changed from yellow to red. No. 8 (E7) The metal part of the hose is gone.

P88: Mistake by the lake No. 1 (A3) The pole now has a flag on it. No. 2 (C3) The white part of the sail showing looks bigger. No. 3 (C8) The hills look slightly different. No. 4 (E1–E2) A silver pole is now yellow. No. 5 (F7) One of the tyres has gone missing. No. 6 (H1–H4) One of the planks has disappeared. No. 7 (H7) There's a big stone that wasn't here before.

P90: Snowy scene No. 1 (A1–B1) That's a new branch. No. 2 (B1) The tree has a red bauble at the top. No. 3 (B3) From brown door to blue door. No. 4 (B5) Someone's built a new house up here. No. 5 (B1–B2) This house is no longer two-tone. No. 6 (B2) A chimney has moved. No. 7 (C3) Someone's on the balcony now. No. 8 (C4) This family no longer have satellite TV. No. 9 (D3) Some curtains have been taken down. No. 10 (E3) The fence has been extended.

P91: What a feast! No. 1 (A1–B1) A metal rod has been removed. No. 2 (B2) Part of the pink hood has gone. No. 3 (B3–B4) Someone's had a haircut. No. 4 (C2) A fork has vanished. No. 5 (C4) That butterfly looks a bit different. No. 6 (D3) Someone's removed some of the words on the packet. No. 7 (D4) The raisins have disappeared. No. 8 (E1) The orange circle on the sole is now black. No. 9 (E4) These socks are now pink all over.

Eye strainers

P94: Man at work No. 1 (A1) There's an extra socket on the woodwork. No. 2 (A2) Someone's lost an eyebrow. No. 3 (A4) One of the wooden posts has disappeared. No. 4 (D1–D2) There's something on the floor that wasn't there before. No. 5 (D2) A red handle has turned blue. No. 6 (C4) There's something new on the side of the bath. No. 7 (E2) A strap on his belt has gone missing. No. 8 (E3) This socket has moved down. No. 9 (E4–E5) The circular object has moved along the floor.

P95: Prickly puzzle No. 1 (A3–B3) A new chimney has appeared on top of the building. No. 2 (A5) A branch has vanished. No. 3 (B1) The cactus on the left has sprouted a flower. No. 4 (C2) The boat wasn't there before. No. 5 (C3) A roof has changed from terracotta to green. No. 6 (D2–E2) This cactus is pointing in a different direction. No. 7 (E4) We've gained a cactus.

P96: Tropical teaser If you look at photo No. 5 closely you will see that a diagonal trunk in the background has vanished.

P97: Cookie confusion Photo No. 1 is different – there's a star cookie in the bottom right with its white stripe facing in the opposite direction from the others.

P98: Gridlock No. 1 (A2) A yellow sign has been removed. No. 2 (A4) A green sign has become a blue sign. No. 3 (B5–C5) There's an extra blue car. No. 4 (C1) One car has moved out of line. No. 5 (C1) And an extra car has appeared beside it. No. 6 (C5–D5) A tree has grown on the verge. No. 7 (D3–D4) A red light has become a yellow light. No. 8 (E5) One car has disappeared completely.

P99: Bubble trouble No. 1 (A2) A big bubble is gone. No. 2 (A5) And a bubble here must have burst. No. 3 (B1–C1) One bubble has grown. No. 4 (B5) A new bubble's appeared from somewhere. No. 5 (C4) The girl now has on a round-neck t-shirt. No. 6 (D3–D4) There's a new bubble on her arm. No. 7 (E1) One bubble is red. No. 8 (E3) A single bubble has become a double bubble. No. 9 (E5) Her hair is shorter.

P100: Fun in the sun No. 1 (A2) A big palm tree leaf has vanished. No. 2 (B2) A third post has appeared on the wall. No. 3 (B3) The wide post has gone. No. 4 (B5–C5) The parasol is now longer. No. 5 (C3) There's something in the corner that wasn't there before. No. 6 (C4) The red ring has become a green ring. No. 7 (D3) This parasol has lost its base. No. 8 (D5) A stool has lost a leg. No. 9 (E2) There's a ring floating in the water that wasn't there before.

P101: Roger Roger No. 1 (A1–B1) The boy's helmet has an extra stripe. No. 2 (B2) A circle's missing from the roof. No. 3 (C2) The microphone has got shorter. No. 4 (C3) The man's hair has grown. No. 5 (C5) Is the yellow band on that stick new? No. 6 (D5) A knob is now red. No. 7 (E3) The yellow stripe on the boy's trousers has disappeared. No. 8 (E4) An extra knob has appeared.

P102: Mask task No. 1 (A3) There's an extra flower on the hat. No. 2 (B1–C1) A yellow flower has become a pink flower. No. 3 (B2) Part of the decoration on the forehead has gone. No. 4 (B5–C5) That street sign wasn't there before. No. 5 (C2) These lips are now red. No. 6 (D3) A leaf has lost a vein. No. 7 (D3) Another leaf has vanished.

P103: Kite-flying conundrum No. 1 (A4–B4) Two tails have become three tails. No. 2 (B2) A yellow section on the purple kite has disappeared. No. 3 (B3) A new kite is in the sky. No. 4 (C3–C4) The teddy kite is pointing the other way. No. 5 (D5) A yellow beak has become an orange beak. No. 6 (E2) Someone in the background has disappeared. No. 7 (E4) A red section on this big kite is now black. No. 8 (E5) Weren't his trousers shorter earlier?

P104: Sweet surprises No. 1 (A2–A4) The chimney is bigger. No. 2 (B4) A green sweet is now blue. No. 3 (C5) There's an extra green bean. No. 4 (D6) Someone's eaten a yellow sweet. No. 5 (E2) The red sweet has disappeared. No. 6 (E4–E5) A white stripe has vanished on the big sweet. No. 7 (E7–F7) A yellow sweet is now blue. No. 8 (F3–G4) There's a second candy cane. No. 9 (F7) There's a new red sweet beside the gingerbread man. No. 10 (G1) There's an extra orange sweet.

P106: Push the boat out No. 1 (A4–B4) There's an extra light. No. 2 (A4–B5) The middle part of the sign has vanished. No. 3 (B1) A beige jacket has become a blue jacket. No. 4 (B4) Something's changed from grey to red. No. 5 (C2–D2) A post has disappeared. No. 6 (C3–D4) The gondolier is facing the opposite way. No. 7 (E1) One of the bands on the post has been removed.

P107: See plane? No. 1 (A2) There's an extra little cloud in the sky. No. 2 (B4) Some trees have grown taller. No. 3 (C1) There's something extra on the wing tip. No. 4 (C3–B4) The white tip of one propellor has vanished. No. 5 (C3–C4) The white section at the side is shorter. No. 6 (D3) The red section is now blue. No. 7 (D5) The top of one of the tyres has changed from black to grey. No. 8 (E2) A black section at the end of one of the floats has vanished. No. 9 (E5) There's an extra plank.

P108: Out of puff A yellow section of balloon at the bottom left is now red in photo No. 6.

P109: Cute as candy Photo No. 2 is different – an orange 'O' in the bottom middle has a hole in it that the others are missing.

P110: Lassie go home! No. 1 (A1) One of the buildings in the background is taller. No. 2 (A2) A purple flower is now a white flower. No. 3 (B3) Lassie's forehead has more of a 'V' shape now. No. 4 (B4–B5) A purple flower has vanished. No. 5 (C3) Lassie has a new collar. No. 6 (C5) A pink flower is no longer there. No. 7 (D3–E3) A pink flower here is now shorter. No. 8 (E1) One little pink flower has become a little yellow flower.

P111: What a catch! No. 1 (A2) An extra chain has appeared. No. 2 (A4–A5) Was that handle there before? No. 3 (B5–C5) The rope has vanished. No. 4 (C3) Looks like that buckle has moved up his strap. No. 5 (C5–D5) A blue glove has become a yellow glove. No. 6 (D4) The white band has been removed. No. 7 (D5) The green box is shorter. No. 8 (E2) And the bucket has an extra handle. No. 9 (E4) The red tool on the floor has disappeared.

P112: Party time No. 1 (A2) A green spot is now blue. No. 2 (A5) This hat has grown. No. 3 (B3–C3) The balloon's lost its bottom. No. 4 (B4) An orange spot is now green. No. 5 (B5) A yellow balloon is now orange. No. 6 (B7) A purple section of this hat is yellow. No. 7 (C4–C5) Someone's had a haircut. No. 8 (C8) The party blower is all white. No. 9 (F3–F4) The green stripe has vanished. No. 10 (G4) A red balloon is gone.

P114: Merry-go-round No. 1 (A2) One light is pink. No. 2 (B2–B3) One decorative section is longer. No. 3 (B4) A light has vanished. No. 4 (C8) This horse has lost part of its mane. No. 5 (E2) A horse has lost a chin-strap. No. 6 (F2–F3) A green band has become a red band. No. 7 (F7) A diagonal stripe has vanished. No. 8 (G3) A horse has lost a hoof. No. 9 (H4) The pole is now shorter.

P116: Whatta lotta pots! No. 1 (B3) One of the leaves is a lot bigger. No. 2 (C1) A pot on the left has vanished. No. 3 (C4) One pot is now terracotta all over. No. 4 (C5) A white and beige pot has vanished. No. 5 (D1–D2) One pot has a new stripe. No. 6 (D4–E4) That pot on the ground wasn't there before. No. 7 (D5) A post has disappeared. No. 8 (E1) This bench has an extra post.

P117: Whoa horsey! No. 1 (A4–B4) The spire is shorter. No. 2 (B2) A signpost has disappeared. No. 3 (C3) The horse has lost a nose-strap. No. 4 (C4) One of the jump posts is shorter. No. 5 (D1) The horse's tail has been cut. No. 6 (D2) The white post has moved slightly to the left. No. 7 (D4) A black stripe on a horizontal plank has vanished. No. 8 (D4) One of the diagonals on the base is gone. No. 9 (D5) The black plantpot is bigger.

P118: Hill city No. 1 (C4) One of the sections of the dome is now plain. No. 2 (D4) The top part of the house below has vanished. No. 3 (E1) There's an extra house on the left. No. 4 (E8) Something's grown on a roof. No. 5 (F3–F4) Two windows have become three windows. No. 6 (F8) This window has expanded. No. 7 (H4) This house is now taller. No. 8 (H6) A doorway has disappeared.

P120: Bright and beautiful One of the flowers on the right of photo No. 4 has lost a red stripe.

P121: Hip-wiggling fun The dancer in photo No. 2 has lost a pompom on the left.

P122: Gnome alone No. 1 (B2) One of the flowers has changed from green to red. No. 2 (B3–B4) Our gnome's hat has changed direction. No. 3 (C5) And he's lost a sideburn on the right. No. 4 (D2) There's an extra red flower to be found. No. 5 (E2) One sleeve has shrunk. No. 6 (F4) The two lines at the front of the gnome's trousers have vanished. No. 7 (F8) What a pretty pink flower. No. 8 (G2) One flower is now taller than before. No. 9 (H5) We've lost a flower at the front.

Ultimate challenges

P126: Hats off No. 1 (A3–A4) One doll has a new bow on her hat. No. 2 (C1) Someone's lost a foot. No. 3 (D2) This hat has a flower that wasn't there before. No. 4 (E3–F3) A pink ribbon has vanished from the front of the dress. No. 5 (E8) The corners of this little doll's mouth have turned down. No. 6 (F3–F5) White lace has become yellow lace. No. 7 (G1) A blue arm has disappeared. No. 8 (G6) This doll's eyes are looking in the opposite direction.

P128: Super structure No. 1 (A2) The tower has got taller. No. 2 (C5) The white structure on top of the building has vanished. No. 3 (D1–D2) A green section is now grey. No. 4 (D2) A window has disappeared. No. 5 (D4) There's an extra window at the bottom. No. 6 (D5) Two windows on the side are no longer there. No. 7 (E1) Someone's parked an extra car. No. 8 (E3) A green section of the building is now black. No. 9 (E3) Isn't that an extra window at the bottom? No. 10 (E4) The side windows have gone. No. 11 (E5) A pillar has also gone.

P129: Chief big mistake No. 1 (B3) The white section between the eyebrows is gone. No. 2 (B3) A new red section has appeared top right. No. 3 (B3) The beak is slightly shorter at the bottom. No. 4 (C1) This wing has a whole extra feather. No. 5 (D2) A green section is now red. No. 6 (D3) A section here has changed from red to green. No. 7 (D5) A black circle with a red middle has vanished. No. 8 (E3) One of the black markings has disappeared.

P130: Good year! In photo No. 1 one of the bottle tops, just below the man's elbow, is more visible.

P131: Jellybean genius Photo No. 5 is the odd one out as a white bean on the left is now orange.

P132: Weird Christmas No. 1 (A3–B3) A pillar has vanished. No. 2 (B2) The pompom on the hat is smaller. No. 3 (C1) A star has disappeared. No. 4 (D2) From red nose to black nose. No. 5 (E2) One of the soldier's stripes has been removed. No. 6 (E4) And someone's lost an eye. No. 7 (G2) A red leg section is now green. No. 8 (G5) One button is no longer there. No. 9 (G8) A new candle has appeared. No. 10 (H8) We have an extra cherry.

P134: Temple trouble No. 1 (A5) An extra flourish appears on the wall here. No. 2 (B1–B2) From two strings of beads to three. No 3 (B3) The horn has got bigger. No. 4 (B4–C4) A little figure has vanished. No. 5 (C1) A blue section is now green. No. 6 (C4) A blue skirt is now a brown skirt. No. 7 (C5) Someone is facing in the opposite direction. No. 8 (D4–E4) This pointed element has grown in size. No. 9 (D5) The crown has lost its top. No. 10 (E3) The triangular section at the front has disappeared.

P135: Excess baggage No. 1 (A1–A2) A green bag has disappeared. No. 2 (A3) A yellow label on a strap has vanished. No. 3 (A3) The same bag has a new logo. No. 4 (B1) The white label is now longer. No. 5 (B2) An extra label has appeared on the green bag. No. 6 (C1) A yellow label on the red case is gone. No. 7 (C4) This bag is no longer leaning to the right. No. 8 (C5) One white stripe has become two white stripes. No. 9 (D5) Someone's removed a black stripe on the white bag. No. 10 (E1) This bag has lost a handle. No. 11 (E2) The green bag has lost a brown square on one handle. No. 12 (E4) This handle has grown. No. 13 (E5) A strap has been removed on the beige bag.

P136: Pick out the penguin One of the penguins in the middle of photo No. 1 is missing the orange stripe on its beak.

P137: Pebbles on the beach In photo No. 2, a grey pebble has become a white pebble, middle bottom.

P138: You're getting warm No. 1 (A3) The boat is facing in the opposite direction. No. 2 (A7–B7) This tree has got taller. No. 3 (E6) One of the squares at the edge of the pool has been reduced. No. 4 (F1) A leaf from this palm tree has been removed. No. 5 (F7) A sun lounger has vanished. No. 6 (G8) A sun lounger is missing an arm. No. 7 (H3) There's someone new on a lounger. No. 8 (H6) A chair has vanished. No. 9 (H7) The parasol has an extra logo. No. 10 (H8) The same parasol has a double pole.

P140: Room with a view No. 1 (A6) The spire is higher. No. 2 (B2–C2) A crumbling tower has disappeared. No. 3 (C6) Two windows have become three windows. No. 4 (D5) A window has moved to the right. No. 5 (D6) Someone's put something blue on top of this roof. No. 6 (E1) The white wall has changed shape. No. 7 (F8) There's a chimney here that wasn't here before. No. 8 (G3) There are two big white chimneys now. No. 9 (E8) A small window has been removed. No. 10 (G8) A red square has vanished.

P142: Tough science No. 1 (A6) We have an extra black ball. No. 2 (C3) A blue ball has become a blue square. No. 3 (F4) A red ball has disappeared. No. 4 (F4) And so has the linking branch between the black and blue balls. No. 5 (F7–F8) We've lost a white branch. No. 6 (G2) A blue ball has become a red ball. No. 7 (G4–H4) The link between the black and red balls has gone. No. 8 (H6–H7) An extra branch is showing between two red balls. No. 9 (H7) A black ball has become a yellow ball.

P144: Touching the sky In photo No. 1 a skyscraper in the middle background has disappeared.

P145: Don't stall for time If you look closely at photo No. 5 you will see that a carrot near the bottom is shorter.

P146: On parade No. 1 (A1) A lantern has vanished. No. 2 (A2) There's a window here that wasn't there before. No. 3 (A4) A four-pane window now has six panes. No. 4 (C2) The policeman has a black stripe on his arm. No. 5 (C5) We've lost a hat in the background. No. 6 (C5) A white belt is now a black belt. No. 7 (D1) An onlooker has lost a bag strap. No. 8 (D2) The horse has lost the strap on its belly. No. 9 (D3–E3) Who moved the pigeon? No. 10 (D3) One of the bandsmen now has on a white shoe.

P147: Shirts off No. 1 (A1–B2) A striped shirt is now a plain white shirt. No. 2 (A4) A tie has vanished. No. 3 (A5) The pole has been extended. No. 4 (B3) An additional orange tie has appeared. No. 5 (D2–E2) A red tie is now a blue No. 6 (D3–E3) A shirt's been turned upside-down. No. 7) A line on the wall has disappeared. No. 8 (E1) A shirt s lost a label. No. 9 (E4) The purple tie has grown. No. 10) Someone's moved the orange item.

P148: Busy beach No. 1 (A5) A beach toy has lost its tail. No. 2 (A5–B5) This boy now has a friend who looks a lot like him. No. 3 (B1) Someone walking is now someone sitting down. No. 4 (B3–C2) A bikini has become a one-ce costume. No. 5 (B3) Red trousers are now blue users. No. 6 (D1–E1) There's a new person to hold ds with. No. 7 (D2–E2) A black swimsuit is now white. , 8 (D5) Two people have vanished. No. 9 (D4–E5) The ch toy now has red spots. No. 10 (E1) Someone's nged direction.

P149: The curtain falls No. 1 (A2) A white bead now has a black middle. No. 2 (A4) Instead of a yellow bead on top of a red bead, we now have a red bead on top of a yellow bead. No. 3 (D2) A long green bead is now blue. No. 4) The brown patterned bead has changed to a plain blue d. No. 5 (D4) A white bead on a strand of green beads s disappeared. No. 6 (D5–E4) Half of the strand on the ht has vanished. No. 7 (E1) A blue bead is now a green d. No. 8 (E4) A red and black bead is now plain black.

First published in Great Britain in 2007 by

Quercus
21 Bloomsbury Square
London
WC1A 2NS

A CIP catalogue record for this book is available from the British Library

ISBN-10: 1 84724 283 9
ISBN-13: 978 1 84724 283 9

Printed and bound in China

10 9 8 7 6 5 4 3 2 1

160

Picture credits

Fotolia:
pp. 25, 28, 29, 32, 33, 38, 39, 44, 46, 56, 66/67, 69, 80, 97, 103, 106, 110, 111, 126/127, 132/133, 146, 147, 148, 149

iStock:
pp. 5, 8, 10, 11, 12/13, 14, 15, 20, 21, 24, 26, 30, 34/35, 36, 37, 42/43, 45, 47, 48/49, 52/53, 54, 55, 57, 58, 59, 60, 61, 62, 63, 64/65, 68, 76/77, 78/79, 84, 86/87, 94, 95, 98, 99, 100, 101, 102, 104/105, 107, 108, 109, 112/113, 114/115, 116, 117, 118/119, 120, 121, 122/123, 128, 129, 130, 131, 134, 135, 136, 137, 138/139, 140/141, 142/143, 144, 145

Nick Clark: pp. 27, 31, 41, 70, 72, 73, 74/5, 85; Martha & Eliza: p.91; Ali Moore: p.40; Judith Shipman: pp.16, 19, 88/89, 96; Austin Taylor: pp. 17, 18, 22, 23, 71, 81, 82/83, 90

Design: Austin Taylor, Keith Miller
Digital image retouching: Ian Atkinson
Editor: Ali Moore for Book Creation Projects